T2-CQC-480

PRIMARY SOURCES IN AMERICAN HISTORY™

THE TRAIL OF TEARS

A PRIMARY SOURCE HISTORY OF THE FORCED RELOCATION OF THE CHEROKEE NATION

ANN BYERS

rosen central
Primary Source™

The Rosen Publishing Group, Inc., New York

*To Frances Cude, who has always inspired me by her pride in her Cherokee heritage,
her love for all people, and her strong faith in God*

Published in 2004 by The Rosen Publishing Group, Inc.
29 East 21st Street, New York, NY 10010

First Edition

Library of Congress Cataloging-in-Publication Data

Byers, Ann.
The Trail of Tears: a primary source history of the forced relocation of the Cherokee Nation/ Ann Byers.—1st ed.
    p. cm. — (Primary sources in American history)
Summary: Uses primary source documents, narrative, and illustrations to recount the history of the U.S. government's removal of the Cherokee from their ancestral homes in Georgia to Oklahoma in 1838.
Includes bibliographical references and index.
ISBN 0-8239-4007-1
1. Trail of Tears, 1838—History—Sources—Juvenile literature. 2. Cherokee Indians—History—Sources—Juvenile literature. 3. Cherokee Indians—Relocation—Juvenile literature. 4. Jackson, Andrew, 1767-1845—Relations with Cherokee Indians—Juvenile literature. 5. United States. Act to Provide for an Exchange of Lands with the Indians Residing in any of the States or Territories, and for Their Removal West of the River Mississippi. [1. Trail of Tears, 1838—History—Sources. 2. Cherokee Indians—History—Sources. 3. Indians of North America—Southern States—History—Sources.]
I. Title. II. Series.
E99.C5B94 2003
973.04'9755—dc21

2002156101

Manufactured in the United States of America

On the front cover: *The Trail of Tears*, a painting by Robert Lindneux. Courtesy of the Woolaroc Museum, Bartlesville, Oklahoma.

On the back cover: First row (left to right): immigrants arriving at Ellis Island; Generals Lee and Grant meet to discuss terms of Confederate surrender at Appomattox, Virginia. Second row (left to right): Lewis and Clark meeting with a western Native American tribe during the expedition of the Corps of Discovery; Napoléon at the signing of the Louisiana Purchase. Third row (left to right): Cherokees traveling along the Trail of Tears during their forced relocation west of the Mississippi River; escaped slaves traveling on the Underground Railroad.

ONTENTS

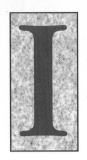NTRODUCTION

The Cherokee lived in what became the United States hundreds of years before the first European set foot in the New World. Related to the Iroquois, they had migrated to the southern Appalachians from the Great Lakes region. Following the American Revolution and the birth of the United States, the Cherokee were considered a separate nation, a country within a country. Though living apart, they were committed to peaceful coexistence with their white neighbors.

A NATION OPPRESSED

Their neighbors, however, were less interested in peace than in land. Pressured by white settlers eager to occupy valuable and productive Cherokee land, the United States government began a long campaign—marked by broken treaties, false promises, racist attitudes, and threats of military force—to move the Cherokee off their territory and out of their homes and to relocate them to the "Great American Desert" west of the Mississippi River.

This was not the first time the Cherokee would be forced off their lands. The white men who came from across the sea had pressed farther and farther into the Cherokee Nation over the years, taking over vast tracts of land as they advanced. Often, the invasion of the white settlers was accompanied by violence. Some of the settlers attacked and robbed the Indians and set their homes and other buildings on fire.

The settlers were not the only ones oppressing the Cherokee. The government of the United States, which had promised to protect the Indians, also treated them cruelly. Repeatedly signing treaties that promised to protect Indian safety and land, even as it took both away, the government broke nearly every vow it made to the Cherokee. By 1838, it was no longer even bothering to make empty promises and vows of friendship. Instead, it was sending in troops with an ultimatum: leave or be removed by force. The expulsion of the Cherokee from their native lands was about to begin. Four thousand Cherokee were about to lose their lives to hunger, cold, and disease during the forced march to Oklahoma. The Cherokee were about to embark on the Trail of Tears.

TIMELINE

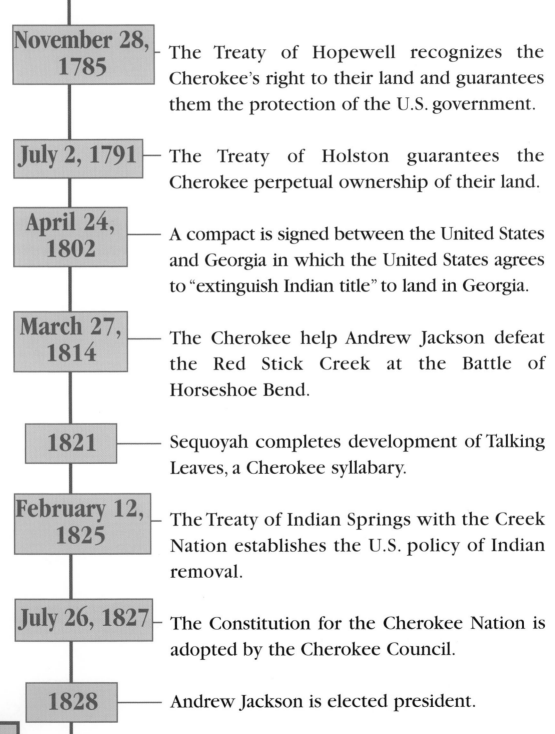

November 28, 1785 — The Treaty of Hopewell recognizes the Cherokee's right to their land and guarantees them the protection of the U.S. government.

July 2, 1791 — The Treaty of Holston guarantees the Cherokee perpetual ownership of their land.

April 24, 1802 — A compact is signed between the United States and Georgia in which the United States agrees to "extinguish Indian title" to land in Georgia.

March 27, 1814 — The Cherokee help Andrew Jackson defeat the Red Stick Creek at the Battle of Horseshoe Bend.

1821 — Sequoyah completes development of Talking Leaves, a Cherokee syllabary.

February 12, 1825 — The Treaty of Indian Springs with the Creek Nation establishes the U.S. policy of Indian removal.

July 26, 1827 — The Constitution for the Cherokee Nation is adopted by the Cherokee Council.

1828 — Andrew Jackson is elected president.

TIMELINE

April 28, 1830 — The Indian Removal Act is signed into law by President Andrew Jackson. The act gives the president the authority to negotiate removal treaties with Indian tribes living east of the Mississippi River.

March 18, 1831 — *Cherokee Nation v. Georgia* declares the Cherokee a "dependent nation."

March 3, 1832 — *Worcester v. Georgia* nullifies Georgia's laws against the Cherokee, but is ignored by Andrew Jackson.

1832 — Georgia's system of land and gold lotteries takes land away from the Cherokee and gives it to white settlers.

December 29, 1835 — The Treaty of New Echota gives up all Cherokee land east of the Mississippi River.

1838–1839 — Trail of Tears—The Cherokee are forced to move to Indian Territory west of the Mississippi.

September 6, 1839 — The new Cherokee Constitution is adopted, and Tahlequah is established as the new capital of the nation.

CHAPTER 1

THE CHEROKEE NATION

When European explorers came to the New World, the Cherokee lived in present-day Georgia, Tennessee, North and South Carolina, West Virginia, and parts of Kentucky and Alabama. They called themselves Ani-Yun-wiya—the Principal People. They were skilled hunters and fearsome warriors.

After their first contact with the white man, however, the Cherokee adopted new ways of living partly in order to more easily coexist with the new settlers and enjoy a higher quality of life. Instead of roaming the forests to hunt deer, elk, bear, and buffalo as they used to do, they began to settle on farms, growing crops and raising livestock. They moved out of their wigwams and built houses of logs, boards, and bricks, like their white neighbors. They learned to turn their cotton into cloth that white settlers would buy. They became farmers and traders instead of warriors and hunters. They even owned African slaves.

Adopting the White Man's Ways

By the early nineteenth century, the Cherokee had adopted the white man's ways to such a great degree that they and the neighboring Creek, Chickasaw, Choctaw, and Seminole were known as the Five Civilized Tribes. The Cherokee was the largest of the five.

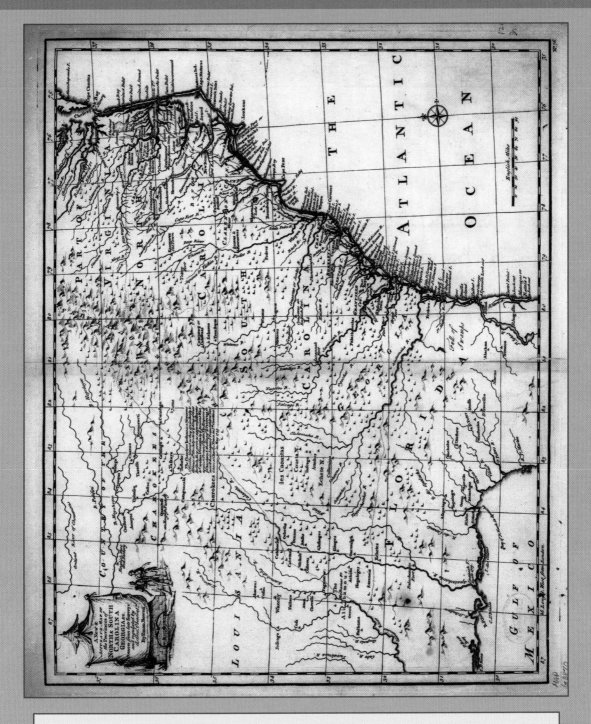

This is a 1747 map by Emanuel Bowen of Florida, Louisiana, North Carolina, South Carolina, and Georgia (the small strip of territory between South Carolina and Florida). It is based on a 1733 map of North America by Henry Popple. Before the Europeans arrived, this land was the home of the Cherokee Nation and several other tribes.

This is the nineteenth-century home of Cherokee chief James Vann. It is one of the oldest remaining structures in north Georgia. Vann lived here with several wives and owned hundreds of acres of farmland around the house, in addition to almost 200 slaves. After Vann's death, the house passed to his son Joe, but the Vanns were forced off their property by the Georgia Guard in March 1835.

One of the leaders of the Cherokee, Chief James Vann, saw that other Indian tribes had completely vanished as white settlements advanced. He believed that the only way his people would survive would be to adapt to the white culture around them. Setting the example that he wanted his people to follow, Vann built a lavish home on his huge plantation, modeled after the great mansions of wealthy whites. His family's clothes were no different from those of any other well-to-do Americans of the early 1800s. Vann also introduced formal European-style education and Christianity to his people. On a visit to Washington in 1800, he met a group of Moravian missionaries (representing a branch of Protestantism) from North Carolina. He invited them to bring both their religion and their schools to the Cherokee.

The schools were open only to children, however. Many adult Cherokees, especially the older ones, could neither read nor write. A Cherokee silversmith named Sequoyah worked for twelve years to develop a system for translating the Cherokee spoken language into a written one. He experimented with different written characters before finally settling, in 1821, on eighty-six symbols, each of which represented a syllable of

Cherokee Alphabet

Sounds represented by vowels.

Consonant Sounds.

The chart at top left shows the syllabary created by the Cherokee scholar and tribal leader Sequoyah *(bottom right)*, in 1821. Sequoyah is shown pointing to a similar chart. He was the first to turn the spoken Cherokee language into a written one. Using a phonetic system, where each sound made in speech was represented by a symbol, he created Talking Leaves, eighty-five letters that make up the Cherokee alphabet.

Cherokee speech. Because the symbols stood for syllables, not individual letters, Sequoyah's system is called a syllabary rather than an alphabet. The Cherokee, thousands of whom were said to have become literate within just a few months of the syllabary's introduction, called it Talking Leaves.

By 1828, the Cherokee Nation had adopted many American institutions and cultural styles. It had a constitution, a national council that made laws, and a system of courts. Its officials were democratically elected by the people. The Cherokee police force—the Lighthorse Patrol—maintained order throughout the nation's lands. The tribal capital in the town of New Echota featured impressive government buildings. A network of roads, schools, churches, and businesses knit the people together, forming an independent nation that looked very much like the white nation that bordered it.

Cherokees and whites were very different in one critical respect, however: the way they viewed land. To the European-descended settlers, land was a means to personal wealth and comfort, something to be bought, sold, and owned by individuals. To the Cherokee, on the other hand, land tended to be viewed as sacred and communal, to be possessed by no single person. It was their home from ancient times and the burial place of their ancestors. The land was the source of their food, their clothing, and their shelter. It gave them life and sustained their existence. It was their protection. The traditional approach dictated that land was not to be parceled out to individuals; it belonged to all.

The first, last, and greatest conflicts between the Cherokee and white men would be over their different conception of the land on which they lived. This difference would drive a wedge between them and lead to unimaginable tragedy.

CHAPTER 2

BROKEN PROMISES

Before the white man came to North America, the Cherokee roamed over 135,000 square miles of the present-day southeastern United States. As the white population along the Atlantic coast grew, settlers began to move west, onto Cherokee land. They cut down trees, killed buffalo, and built homes and villages. Some settled on what appeared to be unoccupied tracts of land, but these were actually the hunting grounds the Indians depended upon for their food.

The Cherokee tried to drive the intruders from their land, and bloody clashes took place all along the eastern edge of Cherokee territory. Still, this eastern edge kept moving steadily westward as more and more whites stole property that had belonged to the Cherokee for hundreds and hundreds of years.

The First Treaty, the First Broken Promise

The Cherokee protested to the new government that had just won its independence from England. In 1785, the United States of America signed an agreement with the "Head-Men and Warriors of all the Cherokees." The Treaty of Hopewell defined very clear boundaries separating Cherokee land from the U.S. territory that was open for settlement. It allowed the Cherokee to deal with trespassers in any way they felt appropriate. The

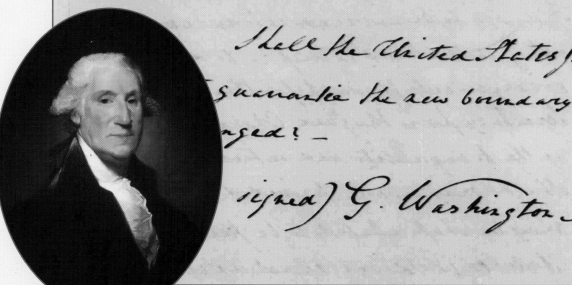

settlement made by the white people six tracts of Hopewell in November 1785?

2 - If so - shall compensation amount of dollars annually or of dollars in gross be made to the Cherokees land they shall relinquish, holding the peers of the land accountable to the United States for its value? -

Shall the United States guarantee the new boundary aged? -

signed) G. Washington

The first treaty the United States made with the Cherokee was also the first treaty it violated. The Treaty of Hopewell, signed in 1785, established the border of Cherokee territory and stated that only Native Americans were allowed to settle on it. By 1790, however, 500 white families had moved onto Cherokee land and built settlements. President George Washington *(inset)*, conscience-striken over this disrespectful treatment of the Cherokee, wrote a letter to the Senate *(shown above)*, alerting them to the treaty violation and stating his intention to enforce the law. See transcript on page 54.

document guaranteed that the Cherokee would be placed under the protection of the United States.

The dispute over territory seemed to have been settled legally. Enforcing the law, however, was difficult. Settlers continued to swarm over the Cherokee borders specified in the treaty and stake their claims to native land. So the Indians appealed to President George Washington. Having placed themselves under the protection of the federal government, the Cherokee referred to Washington and the presidents who succeeded him as their Great White Father. They called themselves his red children. Surely he would right this injustice.

President Washington wanted to enforce the treaty, feeling it was the only right and honorable thing to do. According to the Constitution, the president was responsible for making and enforcing treaties, with the approval of the Senate. Washington wrote to the Senate, asking for suggestions on how to resolve the Cherokee's complaint, while explaining that more than 500 white families had intruded on Cherokee land, openly violating the Treaty of Hopewell.

Hollow Words

The Senate preferred to see a new treaty put in place rather than enforce an old one by removing white settlers from the land they had occupied. In 1791, eleven months after Washington wrote his letter to the Senate, the Treaty of Holston was signed. The Cherokee gave up the land occupied by the settlers, and the government agreed to pay them $1,000 a year for the property (the annual payment was increased to $1,500 in 1792). New territorial borders were drawn, and a strong promise was made to protect remaining

Cherokee land. All land not given away by the treaty was recognized as belonging to the tribe and was protected against all intruders by the full power of the federal government. Furthermore, the United States and the Cherokee agreed that the peace and friendship between them would be "permanent" and "perpetual." For the Cherokee, relinquishing a little land was a small price to pay for such assurances of future security and peace.

Once again, however, the words of the treaty proved hollow. White families continued to stream through the agreed-upon borders. The Cherokee protested again and again. In response, new treaties were made—and again broken. Treaties signed in Philadelphia in 1794 and in Tellico, Tennessee, in 1798 both began "Whereas the treaty made and concluded on Holston River . . . had not been carried into execution" (as quoted in Charles J. Kappler's *Indian Affairs: Laws and Treaties*). In other words, the government was itself admitting that it continued to make new treaties but did not keep any of them.

Each time another of these meaningless documents was signed, more Cherokee land was given away to white settlers. The government paid the Cherokee Nation for the land, but its hunting grounds were shrinking. The Cherokee were being forced farther and farther west. Each time a treaty was signed, each time land was given up, each time the Cherokee fulfilled their end of the bargain, more promises were made and broken by the U.S. government. The 1798 agreement declared that the Cherokee would never have to leave their land. Even as these promises were being made to the Cherokee, however, agreements were being made with others that contradicted those promises.

Confidential.

Gentlemen of the Senate and of the House of Representatives.

As the continuance of the Act for establishing trading houses with the Indian tribes will be under the consideration of the legislature at it's present session, I think it my duty to communicate the views which have guided me in the execution of that act; in order that you may decide on the policy of continuing it, in the present or any other form, or to discontinue it altogether if that shall, on the whole, seem most for the public good.

The Indian tribes residing within the limits of the U.S. have for a considerable time, been growing more & more uneasy at the constant diminution of the territory they occupy, altho' effected by their own voluntary sales: and the policy has long been gaining strength with them of refusing absolutely, all further sale on any conditions, insomuch that at this time, it hazards their friendship, and excites dangerous jealousies & perturbations in their minds to make any overture for the purchase of the smallest portions of their land, a very few tribes only are not yet obstinately in these dispositions. In order peaceably to counteract this policy of theirs, and to provide an extension of territory which the rapid increase of our numbers will call for, two measures are deemed expedient. First, to encourage them to abandon hunting, to apply to the raising stock, to agriculture and domestic manufacture, and thereby prove to themselves that less land & labour will maintain them in this, better than in their former mode of living. the extensive forests necessary in the hunting life, will then become useless, & they will see advantage in exchanging them for the means of improving their farms, & of increasing their domestic comforts. Secondly to multiply trading houses among them, & place within their reach those things which will contribute more to their domestic comfort than the profession of extensive, but uncultivated wilds. experience & reflection will develope to them the wisdom of exchanging what they can spare & we want, for what we can spare and they want. in leading them thus to agriculture, to

At left is a handwritten and confidential message from President Thomas Jefferson—seen at right in an early-nineteenth-century portrait by Gilbert Stuart—to Congress. In it he outlines his strategy for decreasing the amount of land needed and occupied by Indian tribes. By encouraging the Indians to abandon hunting for agriculture and trading, Jefferson hoped to reduce the size of their settlements and land requirements. As a result, the Indians would be more likely, Jefferson reasoned, to sell large forest tracts to the United States for use by white settlers. In this letter, Jefferson also proposes the exploration project that would become the Lewis and Clark expedition. See transcript on page 55.

Mixed Signals

In 1802, President Thomas Jefferson signed a compact, or agreement, with the state of Georgia. It was called a Deed of Articles and Mutual Cession. Cession meant giving up land; mutual cession meant that Georgia agreed to give some of its land to the United States, while the United States in turn gave some of its land to

Georgia. Basically, the state of Georgia gave to the United States territory that became the states of Alabama and Mississippi. In return, the federal government gave Georgia rights to all land contained in the present-day borders of Georgia. The United States agreed to pay Georgia $1,250,000 for the land it was ceding.

Much of the land described in the compact, however, belonged to neither Georgia nor the United States. It belonged to the Cherokee Nation. President Jefferson understood this, so he made the following promise in the fourth article of the agreement: "The United States shall, at their own expense, extinguish, for the use of Georgia, as early as the same can be peaceably effected, on reasonable terms … the Indian title to all … lands within the State of Georgia" (as quoted in Kappler). "Extinguish the Indian title" meant Jefferson intended to nullify all Indian claims to the land, despite the signed treaties that were in place. According to these treaties, the only way to legally negate the Cherokee's title to the land was for the United States to purchase the territory from them. But this time the Cherokee did not want to sell.

Nevertheless, the United States went ahead and paid Georgia for the land it gave up but never owned in the first place. Meanwhile, Georgia waited eagerly for the federal government to remove the Cherokee from the land it promised the state in return. The government had, in effect, made two conflicting promises. It had promised the Cherokee repeatedly and solemnly that it would protect their right to live on their land forever. And it had promised Georgia that it could take possession of the very same land.

Which promise would be kept? Based upon the previous experience with the U.S. government, the Cherokee had little reason to be optimistic or to trust the white man's promise.

CHAPTER 3

The Cherokee encountered Andrew Jackson long before he became president. They first met as allies in the Creek War. Like the Cherokee, the Creek Indians were increasingly weary of white settlements on their land. They were divided on how to resolve the problem. Many of the Creek, knowing the whites were greater in number and in power, wanted to pursue peace through their Great White Father, the U.S. president. One group of Creeks, however, called the Red Sticks—because they painted their war clubs bright red—vowed to kill all the white settlers. In 1813, this group attacked Fort Mims, an American settlement in present-day Alabama, and killed more than 250 people. The governor of Tennessee called out the militia, which was headed by General Andrew Jackson, and the Creek War began. Embarrassed and offended by the actions of the Red Sticks, other Indians joined in the fight against them. In the final battle of the war, the Battle of Horseshoe Bend, Jackson's army included 100 friendly Creeks and 500 Cherokees.

Friendship at Horseshoe Bend

Without his Indian allies, Jackson would probably not have won the Battle of Horseshoe Bend. In fact, without the help of the Cherokee, the general might not have even survived the fight. According to Cherokee oral history, in the midst of the battle

This portrait of President Andrew Jackson reveals the racist and condescending attitude Jackson—and many Americans—had toward Native Americans. Portrayed as the superior Great White Father, the president towers over the small and submissive Indians at his feet and cradled in his arms. Though dependent upon the help of the Cherokee in his war with the Red Stick Creek, Jackson would quickly turn on his former friends and try to seize their lands, forcing them to relocate far from the ever spreading settlements of white Americans.

Cherokee chief Junaluska came upon a Red Sticks warrior about to kill General Jackson. The chief allegedly saved Jackson's life by pounding a tomahawk through the Creek's skull just in time.

Whether or not this story is true, the Cherokee believed that Andrew Jackson was their friend, a bond cemented by their shared battles. While they waited to hear the terms of the surrender that would officially end the Creek War, Jackson praised them:

> You have fought with the Armies of the United States against the hostile Creeks; many of you have fought by my side. I am happy to meet and shake you by the hand, and rejoice with you in the pleasing prospect of returning peace. You have shown yourselves worthy of the friendship of your Father the President of the United States—in battle you have been brave—in friendship steadfast ...I am charged by your father President of the United States to say to you, Chiefs and Warriors, that your conduct has met with his entire approbation [approval].
> —*Jackson's Address to the Cherokee and the Creek, August 4, 1814, Jackson Papers, Roll 11 and Roll 62, Library of Congress*

Friendship Betrayed

Once released, however, the terms of the surrender stunned all the Indians. Jackson demanded as a condition of peace 23 million acres of land, half the holdings of the entire Creek Nation, only a part of which had waged war against the militia. The Cherokee felt that 4 million of those acres actually belonged to them; it was territory that had been disputed between the two tribes before the war. Additional portions of Creek land Jackson wanted were also in dispute, claimed by the Chickasaw and

To perpetuate Peace, and Friendship between the United States, and Cherokee Tribe, or Nation of Indians, and to remove all future causes of dissension which may arise from indefinite territorial boundaries: The President of the United States of America, by Major General Andrew Jackson, General David Meriwether, & Jesse Franklin Esq{s}. Commissioners Plenipotentiary on the one part, & the Cherokee Delegates on the other, covenant and agree to the following Articles & conditions; which when approved by the Cherokee Nation & constitutionally ratified by the Government of the United States,

---

This is the original document that is known as the Treaty of Turkey Town, signed on September 14, 1816, and ratified by the "whole Cherokee nation" on October 4, 1816. Under its terms, 4,000 Cherokee agreed to give up their land in Tennessee in exchange for land in northwest Arkansas. In addition, they would receive $60,000 over a ten-year period. These Cherokee would come to be known and officially recognized by the U.S. government as the Western Cherokee. Over the next two years, more Cherokee would join them, and the number of Western Cherokee swelled to more than 6,000. See transcript on pages 55–56.

Choctaw. These three tribes, valuable allies in the Creek War, protested the terms of surrender almost as strongly as the friendly Creek. While the Creek were given no choice but to sign, the other Indians took their complaints to President James Madison, pleading with him not to take away their lands. Madison adopted a middle course and urged Jackson to try to purchase the land through treaties.

Jackson was angry. In a letter to his wife, he indicated that he thought he had won all the land he was asking for fairly through battle. He met chiefs from the various tribes at the Chickasaw Council House. He attempted to intimidate them by surrounding them with armed soldiers. He tried to bribe them. The Indians, resisted these tactics and held their ground for some time. In the end, however, Jackson got what he wanted. He and nine Cherokee chiefs signed the 1816 Treaty of Turkey Town through which the United States bought 1,300,000 acres from the tribe. A group of about 4,000 Cherokee, convinced they would eventually lose all of their ancient homeland, gave up their property in Tennessee and moved west to Arkansas, joining another group that had relocated earlier for the same reason.

Although only nine Cherokee chiefs signed the treaty, it read, "Ratified at Turkey Town by the whole Cherokee Nation," giving the misleading impression that the nation as a whole had agreed to this deal. This was an early example of the strategy that was to be used for the next twenty years to seize Indian land against the will of most tribe members. Government agents would find a small group of Cherokees who could be frightened, tricked, or bribed into signing away land on behalf of the entire nation. Almost always this tiny group did not legally represent the nation, nor did it reflect the wishes or interests of the overwhelming majority.

Though these strong-arm negotiations made Jackson seem land-hungry, land was not Andrew Jackson's main concern. He had a larger and even more troubling mission. Jackson's goal was to rid the country completely of Indians. As many of his letters and speeches demonstrate, the man who became a national hero by slaughtering Indians believed that the Native Americans were inferior to the European settlers, posed a potential security threat, and hindered white advancement. He wanted to see them removed to unsettled territory west of the Mississippi River, far out of the way of white farmers. In an attempt to prevent Indian violence and to soothe the consciences of more liberal-minded Americans, Jackson claimed that the Indians could not survive surrounded by settlers and would be better off in a faraway land that was theirs alone.

Andrew Jackson called himself "Friend and Brother" of the Indians. When he was elected president in 1829, he became their "Father." He proclaimed in a message to Congress on December 6, 1830, that "toward the aborigines of the country no one can indulge a more friendly feeling than myself" (as quoted in the *Records of the U.S. Senate, 1789–1990*). But in truth, no one was a greater, more determined enemy of the Indian nations than Andrew Jackson.

CHAPTER 4

THE CHEROKEE'S LOSING BATTLE

Andrew Jackson's was not the only voice for Indian removal. Many of the white settlers on the frontier also called for the Indians to relocate west of the Mississippi River. While some families who had long lived as neighbors with the Cherokee and had received assistance from them during hard times were outraged by Jackson's plan, they were in the minority. Those who argued for removal the loudest were Georgia settlers. After the Cherokee were forced to give up land in West Virginia, the Carolinas, and Tennessee, the majority of the Cherokee Nation migrated to Georgia and became concentrated there. The white settlers of that state reminded their leaders that the United States had promised to nullify Indian claims to all property in Georgia. They wanted the federal government to force all Indians living in the state to leave.

Removal West

The government gave the white settlers what they wanted. In 1825, the United States entered into a treaty with a small number of chiefs of the Creek Nation at Indian Springs. The agreement clearly spelled out the new U.S. policy for Native Americans: "That the several Indian tribes within the limits of any of the states of the Union should remove to territory to be designated on the west side of the Mississippi River" (as quoted in Kappler). The treaty gave two official reasons for drafting such a drastic policy: to fulfill its agreement under the Georgia compact and to protect and help the Indians.

The real reason for the new policy, however, was to remove all Indians from land desired by white settlers. At this point in American history, the country west of the Mississippi was considered a wild, uninhabitable wasteland. Few people believed it would ever be settled by "civilized" Americans or fully incorporated into the union. The land was believed to be worthless, and therefore a useful consolation offering to the tribes that would be forced off their rich, traditional lands.

The Cherokee leaders immediately recognized the grave threat to their future existence from this treaty with the Creek. As always, they appealed to the president, their so-called father and protector. The treaty had been negotiated under James Monroe (president from 1817 to 1825), but enforcement was up to the new president, John Quincy Adams (who took office in 1825). Three Cherokee chiefs wrote to Adams, explaining that they "cannot consent to yield another foot of land" (as quoted in Gary E. Moulton's *The Papers of Chief John Ross*). They argued that the removal of the Cherokee would result in their ultimate extinction and asked Adams never to request the removal of tribes who are living in peace with their white neighbors.

Adams soon learned that the treaty had been made without the true consent of all of the chiefs of the Creek Nation, and he had it declared null and void in 1826. He could not

This is one of the many captivity narratives printed in the early nineteenth century that inspired anti-Indian sentiment by sensationalizing stories of Indian attacks upon white settlers. Newspaper articles and books of the time told similarly exaggerated tales. As a result, many Americans strongly supported the U.S. government's attempts to force tribes like the Cherokee off their land and relocate them far away from white settlements. Anti–Indian sentiment and racist attitudes would live on long after the nations and tribes of the southeastern United States had been moved west of the Mississippi River. Well into the twentieth century, Indians were portrayed as bloodthirsty murderers in Hollywood and television westerns.

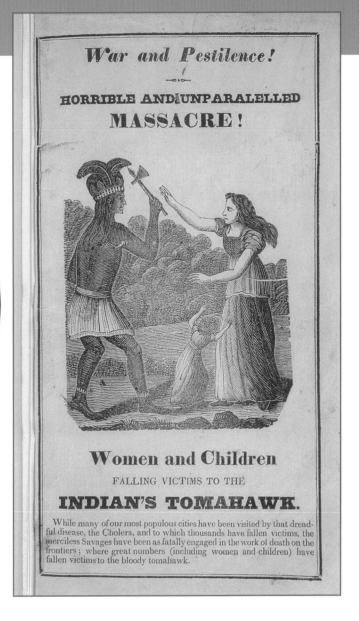

nullify the desires of the citizens of Georgia and of most of the country, however. Most white Americans had decided that the Indians needed to be moved to the "Great American Desert" beyond the Mississippi. That decision was based not only on the lust for Indian land, but also on fear. A number of popular books told false or fictionalized stories of Indian kidnappings and savagery, newspapers sensationalized and exaggerated incidents involving Indians, and broadsides (posters) suggested that Indians were lying in wait, always ready to attack innocent whites.

John Ross, pictured here in an 1843 portrait, was the first and only elected chief of the Cherokee Nation from the time it was formed in 1828 until his death in 1866. Ross was only one-eighth Cherokee (his father was Scottish and his mother was one-quarter Cherokee). John Ross worked hard to try and improve the conditions along the Trail of Tears and is credited with saving many lives. Sadly, Ross's own wife, Quatie, died during the march.

An Embattled Nation Seeks Recognition

Feeling intense and increasing pressure to give up their home-land and move west, the Cherokee leaders knew that the solemn promises made by the U.S. government and contained in their treaties would not protect them. They would have to find a way to protect themselves. Cherokee chiefs reasoned that if they could show the U.S. government—and the state of Georgia—that they were an independent nation, rather than second-class citizens subject to American law and dependent on its protection, they could demonstrate their right to the land they occupied.

As a result, in 1827, the Council of the Cherokee drew up a constitution, elected John Ross to serve as principal chief, and proclaimed to the world what they themselves had always considered to be true: The Cherokee were a sovereign nation. Unimpressed, the state of Georgia ignored the document and continued to push the United States to nullify Indian title to land in the state.

The cry for removal grew even louder in 1828, when gold was found on Indian land. In the next two years, Georgia made

MEMORIAL AND PROTEST

OF THE

CHEROKEE NATION,

To the honourable the Senate and House of Representatives of the United States of North America, in Congress assembled:

THE undersigned representatives of the Cherokee nation, east of the river Mississippi, impelled by duty, would respectfully submit, for the consideration of your honourable body, the following statement of facts: It will be seen, from the numerous subsisting treaties between the Cherokee nation and the United States, that from the earliest existence of this Government, the United States, in Congress assembled, received the Cherokees and their nation into favour and protection; and that the chiefs and warriors, for themselves and all parts of the Cherokee nation, acknowledged themselves and the said Cherokee nation to be under the protection of the United States of America, and of no other sovereign whatsoever; they also stipulated, that the said Cherokee nation will not hold any treaty with any foreign power, individual State, or with individuals of any State: that for, and in consideration of, valuable concessions made by the Cherokee nation, the United States solemnly guaranteed to said nation all their lands not ceded, and pledged the faith of the Government, that "all white people who have intruded, or may hereafter intrude on the lands reserved for the Cherokees, shall be removed by the United States, and proceeded against, according to the provisions of the act, passed 30th March, 1802," entitled "An act to regulate trade and intercourse with the Indian tribes, and to preserve peace on the frontiers." It would be useless to recapitulate the numerous provisions for the security and protection of the rights of the Cherokees, to be found in the various treaties between their nation and the United States. The Cherokees were happy and prosperous under a scrupulous observance of treaty stipulations by the Government of the United States, and from the fostering hand extended over them, they made rapid advances in civilization, morals, and in the arts and sciences. Little did they anticipate, that when taught to think and feel as the American citizen, and to have with him a common interest, they were to be *despoiled by their guardian*, to become strangers and wanderers in the land of their fathers, forced to return to the savage life, and to seek a new home in the wilds of the far west, and that without their consent. An instrument purporting to be a treaty with the Cherokee people, has recently been made public by the President of the United States, that will have such an operation, if carried into effect. This instrument, the delegation aver before the civilized world, and in the presence of Almighty God, is fraudulent, false upon its face, made by unauthorized individuals, without the sanction, and against the wishes, of the great body of the Cherokee people. Upwards of fifteen thousand

On June 21, 1836, John Ross, as chief of the Cherokee Nation, presented to the U.S. Senate and House of Representatives a formal protest of the government's treatment of his people and its increasing tendency toward the breaking of treaties (a printed version of his protest appears above). The protest was signed by 15,000 Cherokee, 90 percent of the nation.

laws that trampled on every right the Cherokee claimed. Georgia pronounced all Cherokee laws "null and void . . . as if the same had never existed," in *Worcester v. Georgia* (1832), and declared the Cherokee subject to state law. Georgia claimed all Cherokee land for itself and forbade the Indians to make or enforce its own laws, hold trials, or testify in any Georgia court. The new laws regulated the lives of the Cherokee so tightly that no white person could go onto Indian land without a permit from the state.

Georgia wasted no time putting the new laws into practice. Surveyors scrambled to divide the territory into sections so that plots could be given out to white Georgians. A land lottery and a gold lottery allowed residents of the state to apply for the newly available land. Settlers' names were put in a drum, and the lucky winners whose names were chosen were given pieces of Cherokee land, including any houses, barns, or other buildings that stood upon them. Sometimes the land was still occupied by Indians who did not find out that the title to their land no longer existed until the white settlers appeared and tried to take possession, often through the use of force.

The Cherokee were horrified by the laws and the brutality with which they were carried out. They could no longer appeal to the president because by then Andrew Jackson held that office (he served from 1829 to 1837), and he was in the process of trying to remove all Indians from their ancestral lands to the unknown wilds west of the Mississippi. Knowing that their "Father," who in 1830 had pushed the Indian Removal Act through Congress, would not protect them, the Cherokee instead turned to the Supreme Court. In the case of *Cherokee Nation v. Georgia* (1831), the Cherokee asked for an injunction to prevent the state from carrying out its new anti-Indian laws.

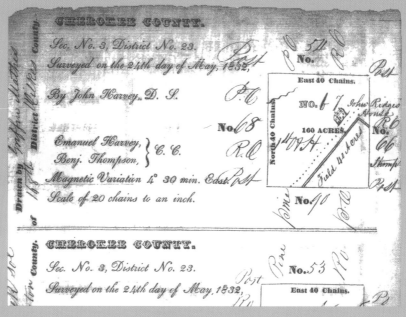

Between 1805 and 1832, Georgia held seven lotteries to distribute to white settlers the land taken from the Cherokee and Creek Indians. Almost three-quarters of the land in present-day Georgia was distributed under this lottery system. Above is a lottery record for a plot of land owned by Major Ridge, a prominent Cherokee leader. The plot also contained Ridge's house *(pictured at top)* in Rome, Georgia.

They argued that the Cherokee Nation was a foreign nation, its sovereignty guaranteed by numerous treaties, and Georgia and its laws had no authority over it.

Chief Justice John Marshall decided that the Cherokee Nation was not a foreign government, but a "dependent nation." Indians, he ruled, were wards of the United States. A ward is someone who is placed under the protection of a court or government. As wards, Marshall argued, the Cherokee could not sue in federal court, and therefore the court could not tell the legislature of Georgia what to do.

The decision was a blow to the Cherokee. They did not win either the injunction or recognition as a sovereign nation. The Cherokee were not through fighting, however. When the white missionary Samuel Worcester was arrested for being in Cherokee territory without a state permit, his arrest became another test of the Georgia laws in U.S. federal courts. This time the Cherokee would win.

In *Worcester v. Georgia* (1832), Chief Justice Marshall declared that the Cherokee was a "distinct community" under the protection of the United States government, governed by treaties, and within that community "the laws of Georgia can have no force." In other words, Georgia did not have the right or the power to make laws for the Cherokee. The anti-Indian laws the state had tried to make were not legal or binding.

When President Jackson heard of the ruling, he is widely rumored to have said, "John Marshall has made his decision; now let him enforce it!" It was Jackson's duty as president to uphold the Court's ruling—to stop Georgia from taking Cherokee land and violating Cherokee rights. But he had no intention of performing that duty. Two years earlier he had succeeded in getting

John Marshall—pictured here in a portrait by John B. Martin—served as chief justice of the Supreme Court for thirty-four years. Under his leadership, the Court would play an important role in determining the fate of the Cherokee Nation. Most of the Court's rulings would go against the Cherokee, but in the 1832 *Worcester v. Georgia* decision, the Marshall Court established an obstacle to Cherokee removal. In this case, Marshall ruled that the Cherokee Nation was sovereign, making the removal laws supported by President Andrew Jackson invalid. Jackson, however, refused to enforce the Court's decision.

Congress to sign the Indian Removal Act. His next actions in this undeclared war against the Indians would be in defiance of the Supreme Court's orders. Jackson was no longer the Cherokee's Great Father. He was now the undisguised champion of their removal—and their destruction.

CHAPTER 5

REMOVAL

For forty-five years, the Cherokee had watched helplessly as acre after acre and mile after mile were whittled from their homeland. Time after time, the trust they placed in the U.S. government and its promises was betrayed as one treaty after another was signed only to be broken. The tribe was forced to give up territory on thirty-six separate occasions between 1785 and 1835. The Cherokee had seen some of their number give in to fear or greed and sell off large parcels of land that belonged to the entire nation. They sensed that white settlers would not rest until they had acquired every last acre of Cherokee territory, and they vowed they would not give up one more foot of land.

Resisting the Indian Removal Act

This sentiment was so strong that the nation reinstated an ancient code: the Blood Law. According to the Blood Law, any Cherokee who attempted to give away land through a treaty with the U.S. government without the approval of the entire Cherokee Nation would suffer death. The Cherokee had signaled—to the U.S. government, to white settlers, and to their own members—that they were deadly serious about retaining what little land they had left.

Andrew Jackson was also interested in reviving an old idea of his: removal of Indians to make room for whites. One of his first actions as president was to ask Congress for an Indian Removal

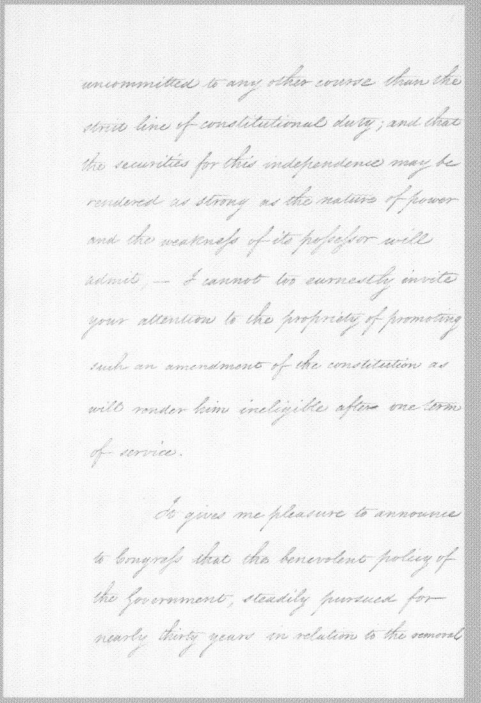

[Handwritten document, left page:]

uncommitted to any other course than the strict line of constitutional duty; and that the securities for this independence may be rendered as strong as the nature of power and the weakness of its possessor will admit, — I cannot too earnestly invite your attention to the propriety of promoting such an amendment of the constitution as will render him ineligible after one term of service.

It gives me pleasure to announce to Congress that the benevolent policy of the Government, steadily pursued for nearly thirty years in relation to the removal

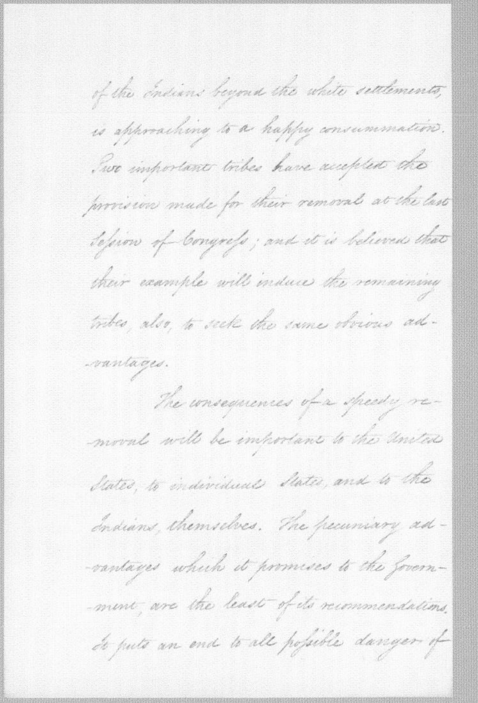

[Handwritten document, right page:]

of the Indians beyond the white settlements, is approaching to a happy consummation. Two important tribes have accepted the provision made for their removal at the last session of Congress; and it is believed that their example will induce the remaining tribes, also, to seek the same obvious advantages.

The consequences of a speedy removal will be important to the United States, to individual States, and to the Indians, themselves. The pecuniary advantages which it promises to the Government, are the least of its recommendations. It puts an end to all possible danger of

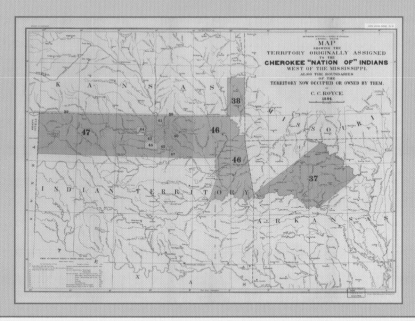

In 1830, President Andrew Jackson sent a message *(top)* to Congress strongly urging for the removal of all Indians to lands west of the Mississippi River and away from white settlements. The map *(bottom)* shows the territory west of the Mississippi originally assigned to the Indians in the 1830s and the far smaller territory they actually occupied or owned by 1884. White settlement continued to spread west after relocation, eating away at Indian territory. For a transcript of Jackson's message to Congress, see page 56.

Act. This legislation, signed in 1830, was different from all previous treaties. It was unilateral (one-sided). It was not a result of negotiation and agreement between the government and an Indian tribe. The Removal Act was not written in consultation with the Indians, but was instead imposed upon them. It said nothing about the government purchasing any land; it said only that the Indians must give up their land east of the Mississippi in exchange for land west of the river. Those who did not wish to relocate would become citizens of the states in which they lived but would have no title to the land on which they currently resided. They would be displaced and made homeless by the influx of white settlers who would claim the land as their own.

The weary Cherokee protested. Their elected principal chief, John Ross, went to Washington several times to try to persuade Andrew Jackson to abandon the removal plan. He wrote to the president again and again, pleading his people's case. Ross appealed to Jackson's sympathy: "Father, your Cherokee children are in deep distress." He appealed to his sense of honor: "Solemn treaty arrangements, made under the Constitution of the United States, are about to be destroyed . . . The Cherokees can now only hang their hopes on the magnanimity and good faith of the United States" (as quoted in *The Papers of Chief John Ross*).

Finally, Ross appealed to a long-standing personal relationship between the Cherokee and Jackson, with the implication that the president owed the nation something:

> Twenty years have now elapsed since we participated
> with you in the toils and dangers of war, and obtained a
> victory over the unfortunate and deluded red foe at
> Tohopekah [Horseshoe Bend], on the memorable 27th

This is a blockhouse, the only remaining structure of what was once Fort Marr, in Benton, Tennessee. Soldiers in the blockhouse could stick their guns out of gunports—holes drilled every two feet along the upper part of the blockhouse—and shoot at attacking enemies. Fort Marr once protected the Cherokee during their war with the Creek. It later served as a stockade to detain the Cherokee before their relocation.

March 1814, that portentous day was shrouded by a cloud of darkness, besprinkled with the awful streaks of blood and death ... We were then your friends ... Now in these days of profound peace, why should the gallant soldiers who in time of war walked hand in hand thro' blood and carnage, be not still friends? We answer, that we are yet your friends.

But Jackson would not budge. The Indian Removal Act had been delivered to Congress, Congress had approved it, and the policy would now be carried out. Five months after the Indian Removal Act was signed, U.S. soldiers began building forts throughout Cherokee territory in which to imprison the Indians in preparation for their removal west.

The Cherokee Divided

With the forts serving as constant reminders of the government's intentions and with continual harassment from the Georgia Guard (a state militia), a small group of Cherokee began to think that compliance with Jackson's wishes might be the only way to prevent the destruction of the entire Cherokee Nation. This group was led by Major Ridge, a very influential leader once strongly opposed to removal. The Ridgites tried to convince the Cherokee that they would never be safe as long as they stubbornly insisted on staying on their ancient land. Ridge's group became known as the Treaty Party because its members wanted to negotiate a treaty with the government rather than resist removal. Given that removal seemed inevitable, they thought they should try to gain as many concessions as possible in a treaty. Without a treaty, they would still be forced to leave their land, but would receive nothing in return.

The Cherokee people were bitterly divided. The huge majority belonged to the Ross faction. They stood united behind their chief, John Ross, hoping his pleas to the president, the Congress, and the American people would somehow enable them to remain where they were, in their own homes and on their own land. The far smaller Ridge faction sent its own delegates to Washington, in an attempt to make the best possible arrangements for what they felt was the inevitable move west.

The Treaty of New Echota

While Andrew Jackson was refusing to speak further with Ross, his agents were meeting with Ridge. On December 29, 1835, twenty members of the Treaty Party gathered with Jackson's representatives in the home of Elias Boudinot (former editor of the *Cherokee Phoenix* newspaper) in New Echota, Georgia. There they signed a document that gave up all Cherokee lands and possessions east of the Mississippi River in exchange for a payment of $5 million and 7 million acres of the "Great American Desert" west of the river.

Though the Cherokee Nation was overwhelmingly opposed to relocation, a very small minority felt it was inevitable and tried to cut the best deal possible with the U.S. government. In December 1835, the government sought out this minority to draft a treaty at New Echota, Georgia. Fewer than 500 Cherokee were there, and none of them were elected officials of the Cherokee Nation. Twenty signed the treaty *(shown at right)*, giving up all Cherokee territory east of the Mississippi to the United States, in exchange for $5 million and new homelands in Indian Territory. More than 15,000 Cherokee protested the illegal treaty to no avail. See transcript on page 57.

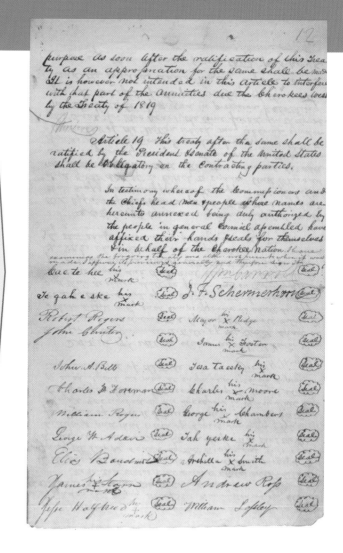

The men who signed the Treaty of New Echota knew that what they were doing was extremely unpopular among the Cherokee. Major Ridge, aware of the Blood Law of his people, is widely reported to have said prophetically, "I have signed my death warrant." But the signers all sincerely believed that they were doing what was best for the Cherokee Nation. They were convinced that relocating to a large wide-open country where they would be free of harassment was their only hope for survival as a people and as a nation.

Most Cherokee, however, felt betrayed. The Treaty Party was not authorized by the Cherokee Council to negotiate on behalf of the nation. The Ridgites did not represent the desires of the overwhelming majority of the Cherokee. The members of the Treaty Party had violated an ancient, sacred law forbidding anyone to give away land that belonged to the entire tribe. Trying to discredit the authority of Ridge, Ross collected and brought to the Senate the signatures of almost 16,000 Cherokee who opposed the action of the twenty who had signed the treaty.

Ross was powerless, however, against a determined Andrew Jackson. The president pushed the U.S. Senate hard, and the treaty was ratified (approved) by just one vote. Five days later, on May 23, 1836, Jackson signed the Treaty of New Echota. According to the terms of the treaty, the Indians had until May 23, 1838—two years from the day the treaty became law—in which to move west voluntarily. The members of the Treaty Party who had signed the treaty moved immediately, knowing their lives were threatened by their fellow Cherokee who felt betrayed. Other Cherokee who were not members of Ridge's group nevertheless believed that moving to Indian Territory across the Mississippi was inevitable. About 2,000 of them joined the Ridgites in moving west.

The Cherokee remaining behind in Georgia vowed never to leave willingly. They hoped Ross could somehow work a miracle. He did not stop writing letters, visiting Washington, and making appeals. In early May 1838, however, when 7,000 U.S. soldiers descended on the Cherokee, the people knew their cause was hopeless.

CHAPTER 6

"THE TRAIL WHERE THEY CRIED"

Throughout the eight years following the passage of the Indian Removal Act into law, the Cherokee were reminded daily of their impending fate. By 1838, only 2,000 Cherokee had migrated west, leaving 16,000 still occupying their ancestral lands. This land became dotted with forts ready to house them in preparation for their forced migration west. Army officers and federal agents roamed the countryside, reminding the Cherokee how little time they had left. White lottery winners began to occupy Cherokee homes and farm their fields. Every day the Cherokee were confronted with the fact of their eventual expulsion from their own country. When the deadline for removal finally came, however, its arrival still seemed sudden.

General Winfield Scott

Though there were some prominent voices raised against removal—including Senators Daniel Webster and Henry Clay; frontiersman and congressman Davy Crockett; and General John Wool, the man first chosen to oversee the removal who resigned in protest—no one could now stop the process that had been started. Two weeks before the deadline for voluntary removal, General Winfield Scott rode up to the Cherokee agency in

Before being asked to replace General John Wool in supervising the removal of the Cherokee Nation to lands west of the Mississippi River, General Winfield Scott had fought in many American conflicts, including the War of 1812, the Mexican-American War, and various wars with the Seminole and Blackhawk tribes. After personally accompanying a group of Cherokee on their westward journey, he returned to Washington, D.C., in 1839. He would go on to serve briefly as a Union general in the Civil War, at the age of seventy-five. He is pictured here in an 1847 portrait by Currier & Ives.

Calhoun, Georgia, with 7,000 soldiers. He pleaded with the Indians to cooperate with him as he moved them west. He told them they had no choice; attempts at resistance or escape would be doomed to failure. He begged them not to fight and not to run. If they did, he warned, "the blood of the white man or the blood of the red man may be spilt." It would almost certainly be impossible "to prevent a general war and carnage" (as quoted in *Niles' National Register*).

Scott was a battle-hardened general, but he was not unfeeling. He issued very clear orders to his troops to treat the Indians with dignity, respect, and kindness. He commanded that anyone who witnessed a fellow soldier treat any Cherokee with harshness or cruelty was to report the incident immediately so the offending soldier could be punished. He ordered that Cherokee families be kept together and the sick and weak be treated with special care. Scott required that all the Cherokee be given meat and flour or corn to sustain them during the journey.

When the roundup began, however, the general's orders were not always followed. Scott could not control the violent and often murderous Georgia Guard that carried out many of the roundup operations. Members of the guard often treated the Cherokee with violence and stole what the Cherokee were forced to leave behind and what little they carried with them, including food that was already in desperately short supply.

A Brutally Successful Operation

In May and June of 1838, the Cherokee were dragged from their homes and forced at bayonet point into the overcrowded forts the army had built eight years earlier. Most were not given time to gather any food or possessions. All weapons were taken from the Indians, allegedly to be returned when the removal was complete and the Cherokee were relocated in their new western home. Some of the people were hurt and abused by the soldiers. Occasionally, white settlers and former neighbors would leap to the defense of Cherokee being mistreated by the Georgia Guard.

Only about 1,000 Cherokee managed to escape, hiding in the hills of North Carolina and Tennessee. Within just two weeks of the beginning of the removal operation, every Cherokee in north Georgia, Tennessee, and Alabama had been captured or killed or had run and hid. With brutal efficiency, the land had been cleared for white occupation.

The forts that housed the Indians while they waited to travel west were little more than holding pens. The government had underestimated the cost of Indian removal and the length of time the Indians would be imprisoned in the forts (which was up to five months). As a result, there was a severe shortage of food, made even worse when soldiers sold food intended for the Cherokee to local settlers. The forts did not provide enough room for so many people. They did not have adequate facilities for sanitation, and human waste collected in living areas. Disease was rampant, including measles, whooping cough, and dysentery (an intestinal disorder marked by severe diarrhea and bleeding). Hundreds died in the removal forts before the journey even began. Some estimates say that a third of the 4,000 deaths resulting from removal occurred in the filthy, dangerous forts. Some estimates for removal-related deaths range as high as 8,000.

The Trail of Tears

Anxious to be finished with his distasteful assignment, General Scott sent three detachments west in June, totaling about 2,800 Cherokee. Each group included a military officer and two physicians. They traveled by steamship and keelboat along the Tennessee, Ohio, Mississippi, and Arkansas Rivers and then walked or rode in wagons the rest of the way. The summer of 1838 was extremely hot, and a drought had lowered the river levels. Some of the boats got stuck on sandbars, and the Indians in those vessels had to be crowded into other, already full boats. Hundreds died on these overcrowded boats without ever reaching the new life they had been promised.

While the first three groups were leaving, John Ross was in Washington, making his final unsuccessful appeal to halt removal.

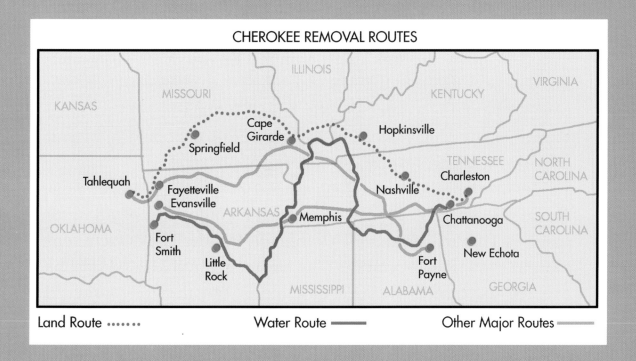

CHEROKEE REMOVAL ROUTES

Land Route ·······   Water Route ———   Other Major Routes ═══

The term "Trail of Tears" actually refers to several different land and water routes taken by the Cherokee and other Indian tribes from their ancestral lands to the new territory in present-day Oklahoma. As this map shows, the most common overland route began in Tennessee and swung north into southwestern Kentucky and southern Illinois. After crossing the Mississippi River, the Cherokee on this trail continued across southern Missouri and the northwest corner of Arkansas into Oklahoma. Road conditions, illness, and harsh winter weather made death a daily occurrence. As many as 8,000 Indians are thought to have died during the entire removal process and its aftermath. Roughly 4,000 Cherokee died on the trail itself.

Upon his return, he was horrified to hear how his people had been treated. He asked General Scott to allow him to organize the remainder of the operation. The general agreed. Ross divided the captives still in the forts into thirteen detachments, each placed under the command of a Cherokee leader. After the difficulties experienced by the first three groups, General Scott postponed the journeys of the last thirteen until September, when the weather would be cooler and the drought might be broken. They would go overland instead of by water so they could hunt and provide themselves with desperately needed food.

The drought did not end, however, until late September. That meant the final stage of the removal could not begin until October. The first group left October 1, but the last detachment did not start until December. The thirteen Cherokee-led groups avoided the oppressive heat of summer, but they encountered other problems equally severe. By November, winter weather had arrived, and the frozen rivers were impossible to cross. Food was scarce. People who were forced to huddle together for warmth also passed their sicknesses along.

The pain and misery of the journey are impossible to describe. Thousands of Cherokee had no blankets. Many had no shoes. The people were starving. As many as twenty Cherokee died a night from pneumonia or the cold. Many who could no longer summon the strength to continue walking simply sat by the side of the trail and waited for death to come for them.

By the time the last of the Cherokee reached their destination, they had walked or sailed from Georgia through parts of Tennessee, Alabama, Mississippi, Kentucky, Illinois, Missouri, and Arkansas, finally ending up in Oklahoma Territory (ten different routes are collectively known as the Trail of Tears).

Several thousand unmarked graves lay between Ross's Landing in Chattanooga, Tennessee (where some of the Cherokee boarded steamships to begin the water route of the journey), and Indian country in Oklahoma Territory. Death came in the form of starvation, exposure to the elements, and disease. The Cherokee call this journey *Nunnadautsun't*—The Trail Where They Cried. It is more often remembered as the Trail of Tears.

CHAPTER 7

THE TRAIL'S END

The Trail of Tears ended in a barren tract of land in Oklahoma Territory. When the 12,000 Cherokee who survived the three- to six-month relocation arrived, they encountered a large group of Cherokee known as the Old Settlers (or Western Cherokee) who had moved west from Arkansas in the 1820s. The 6,000 Old Settlers were not happy about suddenly having to share their resources and power with a new group twice their size. In addition, the Ridgites had also settled in the new territory, along with another 2,000 Cherokee who had voluntarily left with them.

Old Divisions, Fresh Violence

The new Cherokee arrivals (who became known as the New Settlers, or Eastern Cherokee) brought their government and their politics with them. They assumed John Ross was the principal chief of the entire nation—of their party arriving from the east and of the old group already in the west. The Old Settlers, however, had their own chief and their own codes. Tensions developed, and then violence, which erupted quickly and cruelly. Whether in loyalty to Ross or in obedience to the ancient Blood Law, a number of Ross followers took action against the Ridgites less than a month after reaching their new homes. In a single day, they brutally assassinated three of the four primary signers of the Treaty of New Echota—Major Ridge, his son John, and

General Stand Watie, shown here in a photograph from c. 1860–1865, was a member of the Ridge faction that supported Cherokee removal. At the beginning of the Civil War, Watie joined the Southern cause and raised a regiment of Cherokee to serve in the Confederate army. He was the only Indian to achieve the rank of general in the Civil War. Watie surrendered on June 23, 1865, the last Confederate general to lay down his arms.

Elias Boudinot. (Stand Watie, the fourth primary treaty signer, escaped after a messenger warned him of the assassinations.) Chief Ross immediately sent a letter to the general at the nearest fort, asking him to help prevent further bloodshed.

The savagery did not stop, however. The only major treaty signer to escape death, Watie became the leader of a faction strongly opposed to John Ross. It included many of the Old Settlers and the Ridgites. Disagreements between the two groups often erupted in bloody clashes. In one nine-month period, thirty-three murders were reported. The violence raged for seven years before the warring factions realized that unity, not division, was crucial to Cherokee survival. Neither side wanted to see any further suffering or loss of life among the Cherokee. Both knew that to be strong the nation needed to stay as large as possible. So, in 1846, the opposing factions signed a treaty that recognized the Cherokee as one group. John Ross and Stand Watie, enemies for eleven years, shook hands.

A Nation Survives Continuing Adversity

The next fifteen years—before the Civil War divided the country as well as the Cherokee—were a period of relative peace and comfort. During the early years in Oklahoma, the Cherokee laid strong foundations for their new life. The Old and New Settlers joined to create a new constitution. They established a capital in Tahlequah, a city roughly at the geographic center of the nation. They founded public and mission (church-run) schools and built houses, roads, churches, and businesses. A newspaper was established. Cherokee doctors, dentists, and lawyers opened practices. At last, it seemed, the Cherokee people were becoming prosperous and safe from the white man's greed, violence, and deceit.

This is an 1875 photograph of the Cherokee Female Seminary, in Park Hill, Oklahoma, near the Cherokee Nation capital of Tahlequah. Religious schools like this one were constructed and operated by the Cherokee, generally without any U.S. government aid or oversight. The women shown here are from the graduating class of 1875.

Sadly, this period of halting success, stability, and security was not to last long. The Civil War again drove a wedge through the Cherokee Nation, with the New Settlers generally siding with the Confederacy and the Old Settlers fighting for the Union. The Cherokee were heavily involved in the guerrilla warfare raging in Oklahoma and lost as much as a third of their already depleted population during the war.

After the confusion of the Civil War and the continued westward movement of the country's white population, old treaties

The Cherokee National Historical Society was established in 1963 by Chief W. W. Keeler. It is committed to preserving the history and culture of the Cherokee and educating the public about this proud nation. This work is done mainly through the Cherokee Heritage Center *(pictured above)*, in Park Hill, Oklahoma. In addition to a permanent Trail of Tears exhibit and other temporary exhibits, the center's Cherokee National Museum also features the Cherokee National Archives, where Cherokee Nation documents are stored, including historical records, photographs, and legal documents. The center also has an outdoor amphitheater, replicas of ancient and rural villages and farms, and a genealogical library.

were again broken and new treaties were imposed upon the Cherokee. Still more land was taken away—so railroads could be built, so the ever growing and expanding population of whites could spread into and settle western lands, so other relocated Indians would have a place to live. By 1880, there were more whites than Indians in Indian Territory. In 1895, the Curtis Act was passed, which forced the Cherokee to dissolve their tribal government and divide the land that belonged to the entire tribe among individual Cherokees, breaking up the nation. Much of this individually owned land was soon lost to swindling white settlers.

The Cherokee Nation was officially dissolved on March 3, 1906, following a failed attempt by the five tribes to form a state in eastern Oklahoma. The Cherokee people now lived on less than one-third of 1 percent of the 7 million acres granted to them by the Treaty of New Echota. The Cherokee became U.S. citizens and citizens of the new state of Oklahoma.

Still, the people fiercely clung to their identity as Cherokees. They reformed themselves as a nation in 1948. In 1963, the Cherokee National Historical Society was founded, and a museum was established twelve years later. Cherokee festivals and holidays were again celebrated. Today, as then, the Cherokee people are proud of their heritage.

In 1988–1989, the Cherokee Nation observed the 150th anniversary of the beginning of the Trail of Tears and the arrival in Indian Territory. Though nearly broken in body and spirit by the harsh, deceitful treatment by people of the United States and their government and the forced march of the Trail of Tears, the Cherokee Nation has survived and continues to stand tall, with great pride, dignity, and strength. As Principal Chief Chadwick "Corntassel" Smith said in his report to the people in 2002, "History knows of no greater story of a nation facing adversity, surviving, adapting, prospering, and excelling."

PRIMARY SOURCE TRANSCRIPTIONS

Page 14: Excerpt of Letter from President George Washington to the United States Senate Concerning the Cherokee, August 11, 1790

Transcription
To the Senate relative to the Cherokee nation of Indians
United States, August 11, 1790

Gentlemen of the Senate, . . .

During the last year I laid before the Senate a particular ftatement [statement] of the case of the Cherokees. By a reference to that paper it will appear that the United States formed a treaty with the Cherokees in November 1785. That the said Cherokees thereby placed themselves under the protection of the United States, and had a boundary afsigned [assigned] them.

On August 11 the Senate resolved that the treaty at Hopewell with the Cherokees be carried into execution at the discretion of the President, and that the Senate guarantee the Cherokee boundary...

That the White people settled on the frontiers had openly violated the faid [said] boundary by intruding on the Indian lands.

That the United States in Congrefs [Congress] afsembled [assembled] did on the first day of September 1788 ifsue [issue] their proclamation forbidding such unwarrantable intrusions and injoining all those who had settled upon the hunting grounds of the Cherokees to depart with their families and effects without the lofs [loss] of time, as they would anfwer [answer] their disobedience to the injunctions and prohibitions exprefsed [expressed], at their peril.

But information has been received that notwithftanding [notwithstanding] the said treaty and proclamation upwards of five hundred families have settled on the Cherokee Lands exclusively of those settled between the fork of French Broad and Holstein Rivers mentioned in the faid [said] treaty...

I shall conceive myself bound to exert the powers entrusted to me by the Conftitution [Constitution] in order to carry into faithful execution the treaty of Hopewell, unlefs [unless] it shall be thought proper to attempt to arrange a new boundary with the Cherokees embracing the fettlements [settlements], and compensating the Cherokees for the cefsions [cessions] they fhall [shall] make on the occasion. On this point therefore I state the following questions and request the advice of the Senate thereon.

1st. Is it the judgment of the Senate that overtures shall be made to the Cherokees to arrange a new boundary fo [so] as to embrace the fettlement [settlement] made by the white people since the treaty of Hopewell in November 1785?

2. If so, shall compensation to the amount of dollars annually or of dollars in grofs [gross] be made to the Cherokees for the land they shall relinquish, holding the occupiers of the land accountable to the United States for its value?

3dly. Shall the United States ftipulate [stipulate] folemnly [solemnly] to guarantee the new boundary which may be arranged?
signed G. Washington

Page 17: Excerpt of President Thomas Jefferson's Confidential Message to Congress Concerning Relations with the Indians, January 18, 1803

Transcription
Confidential

Gentlemen of the Senate, and of the House of Representatives: …
The Indian tribes residing within the limits of the United States, have, for a considerable time, been growing more & more uneasy at the constant diminution of the territory they occupy, altho' effected by their own voluntary sales: and the policy has long been gaining strength with them, of refusing absolutely all further sale, on any conditions; insomuch that, at this time, it hazards their friendship, and excites dangerous jealousies & perturbations in their minds to make any overture for the purchase of the smallest portions of their land. a very few tribes only are not yet obstinately in these dispositions. In order peaceably to counteract this policy of theirs, and to provide an extension of territory which the rapid increase of our numbers will call for, two measures are deemed expedient. First, to encourage them to abandon hunting, to apply to the raising stock, to agriculture and domestic manufacture, and thereby prove to themselves that lefs [less] land & labor will maintain them in this, better than in their former mode of living. the extensive forests necefsary [necessary] in the hunting life, will then become uselefs [useless], & they will see advantage in exchanging them for the means of improving their farms, & of increasing their domestic comforts. Secondly: to multiply trading houses among them, & place within their reach those things which will contribute more to their domestic comfort, than the pofsefsion [possession] of extensive, but uncultivated wilds. experience & reflection will develope to them the wisdom of exchanging what they can spare & we want, for what we can spare and they want. in leading them to agriculture, to manufactures, & civilization; in bringing together their & our settlements, and in preparing them ultimately to participate in the benefits of our governments, I trust and believe we are acting for their greatest good…The legislature, reflecting on the late occurrences on the Mississippi, must be sensible how desirable it is to pofsefs [possess] a respectable breadth of country on that river, from our Southern limit to the Illinois at least; so that we may present as firm a front on that as on our Eastern border. we pofsefs [possess] what is below the Yazoo, & can probably acquire a certain breadth from the Illinois & Wabash to the Ohio; but between the Ohio and Yazoo, the country all belongs to the Chickasaws, the most friendly tribe within our limits, but the most decided against the alienation of lands. the portion of their country most important for us is exactly that which they do not inhabit. their settlements are not on the Mississippi, but in the interior country. they have lately shown a desire to become agricultural; and this leads to the desire of buying implements & comforts. in the strengthening and gratifying of these wants, I see the only prospect of planting on the Mississippi itself, the means of its own safety. Duty has required me to submit these views to the judgment of the legislature; but as their disclosure might embarras & defeat their effect, they are committed to the special confidence of the two houses.

Page: 22: Excerpt of Treaty with the Cherokee, 1816 (Also Known as the Treaty of Turkey Town)

Transcript
To perpetuate peace and friendship between the United States and Cherokee tribe, or nation, of Indians, and to remove all future causes of dissension which may arise from indefinite territorial boundaries, the president of the United States of America, by major general Andrew Jackson, general David Meriwether, and Jesse Franklin esquire, commissioners plenipotentiary on the one

part, and the Cherokee delegates on the other, covenant and agree to the following articles and conditions, which, when approved by the Cherokee nation, and constitutionally ratified by the government of the United States, shall be binding on all parties:

ART. 1. Peace and friendship are hereby firmly established between the United States and Cherokee nation or tribe of Indians.

ART. 2. The Cherokee nation acknowledge the following as their western boundary: South of the Tennessee river, commencing at Camp Coffee, on the south side of the Tennessee river, which is opposite the Chickasaw Island running from thence a due south course to the top of the dividing ridge between the waters of the Tennessee and Tombigby rivers, thence eastwardly along said ridge, leaving the head waters of the Black Warrior to the right hand, until opposed by the west branch of Well's Creek, down the east bank of said creek to the Coosa river, and down said river.

ART. 3. The Cherokee nation relinquish to the United States all claim, and cede all title to lands laying south and west of the line, as described in the second article; and, in consideration of said relinquishment and cession, the commissioners agree to allow the Cherokee nation an annuity of six thousand dollars, to continue for ten successive years, and five thousand dollars, to be paid in sixty days after the ratification of the treaty, as a compensation for any improvements which the said nation may have had on the lands surrendered...

In testimony whereof, the said commissioners and undersigned chiefs and delegates of the Cherokee nation, have hereto set their hands and seals. Done at the Chickasaw council house, this fourteenth day of September, in the year of our Lord one thousand eight hundred and sixteen.

Page 35: Excerpt of President Andrew Jackson's Message to Congress on Indian Removal, Dated December 6, 1830

Transcript

It gives me pleasure to announce to Congrefs [Congress] that the benevolent policy of the Government, steadily pursued for nearly thirty years, in relation to the removal of the Indians beyond the white settlements is approaching to a happy consummation. Two important tribes have accepted the provision made for their removal at the last session of Congrefs [Congress], and it is believed that their example will induce the remaining tribes, also, to seek the same obvious advantages.

The consequences of a speedy removal will be important to the United States, to individual States, and to the Indians, themselves. The pecuniary advantages which it promises to the Government, are the least of its recommendations. It puts an end to all pofsible [possible] danger of collision between the authorities of the General and State Governments on account of the Indians. It will place a dense and civilized population in large tracts of country now occupied by a few savage hunters. By opening the whole territory between Tennessee on the north and Louisiana on the south to the settlement of the whites it will incalculably strengthen the southwestern frontier and render the adjacent States strong enough to repel future invasions without remote aid. It will relieve the whole State of Mississippi and the western part of Alabama of Indian occupancy, and enable those States to advance rapidly in population, wealth, and power. It will separate the Indians from immediate contact with settlements of whites; free them from the power of the States; enable them to pursue happiness in their own way and under their own rude institutions; will retard the progress of decay, which is lessening their numbers, and perhaps cause them gradually, under the protection of the Government and through the influence of good counsels, to cast off their savage habits and become an interesting, civilized, and Christian community.

What good man would prefer a country covered with forests and ranged by a few thousand savages to our extensive Republic, studded with cities, towns, and prosperous farms embellished with all the improvements which art can devise or industry execute, occupied by more than 12,000,000 happy people, and filled with all the blessings of liberty, civilization and religion?

Page 39: Excerpt of Treaty with the Cherokee, 1835 (Also Known as the Treaty of New Echota)

Transcript

Articles of a treaty, concluded at New Echota in the State of Georgia on the 29th day of Decr. 1835 by General William Carroll and John F. Schermerhorn commissioners on the part of the United States and the Chiefs Head Men and People of the Cherokee tribe of Indians …

Article 1. The Cherokee nation hereby cede relinquish and convey to the United States all the lands owned claimed or possessed by them east of the Mississippi river…

Article 6. Perpetual peace and friendship shall exist between the citizens of the United States and the Cherokee Indians…

Article 8. The United States also agree and stipulate to remove the Cherokees to their new homes and to subsist them one year after their arrival there and that a sufficient number of steamboats and baggage-wagons shall be furnished to remove them comfortably, and so as not to endanger their health, and that a physician well supplied with medicines shall accompany each detachment of emigrants removed by the Government…

Article 16. It is hereby stipulated and agreed by the Cherokees that they shall remove to their new homes within two years from the ratification of this treaty and that during such time the United States shall protect and defend them in their possessions and property and free use and occupation of the same and such persons as have been dispossessed of their improvements and houses…

Article 18. Whereas in consequence of the unsettled affairs of the Cherokee people and the early frosts, their crops are insufficient to support their families and great distress is likely to ensue and whereas the nation will not, until after their removal be able advantageously to expend the income of the permanent funds of the nation it is therefore agreed that the annuities of the nation which may accrue under this treaty for two years, the time fixed for their removal shall be expended in provision and clothing for the benefit of the poorer class of the nation and the United States hereby agree to advance the same for that purpose as soon after the ratification of this treaty as an appropriation for the same shall be made. It is however not intended in this article to interfere with that part of the annuities due the Cherokees west by the treaty of 1819.

Article 19. This treaty after the same shall be ratified by the President and Senate of the United States shall be obligatory on the contracting parties.

In testimony whereof, the commissioners and the chiefs, head men, and people whose names are hereunto annexed, being duly authorized by the people in general council assembled, have affixed their hands and seals for themselves, and in behalf of the Cherokee nation.

I have examined the foregoing treaty, and although not present when it was made, I approve its provisions generally, and therefore sign it.

Wm. Carroll,
J. F. Schermerhorn.

Major Ridge	Andrew Ross	Charles F. Foreman
James Foster	William Lassley	William Rogers
Tesa-ta-esky	Cae-te-hee	George W. Adair
Charles Moore	Te-gah-e-ske	Elias Boudinot
George Chambers	Robert Rogers	James Starr
Tah-yeske	John Gunter	Jesse Half-breed
Archilla Smith	John A. Bell	

GLOSSARY

animosity   Feelings of extreme dislike and hostility toward someone or something.

bayonet   Swordlike blade attached to the barrel of a rifle or musket for close fighting.

carnage   Excessive blood and killing.

cession   Act of giving up, or ceding, land.

drought   Period of time with little or no rain.

extinguish   To make extinct, or to completely wipe out.

grievance   Complaint because of a wrong suffered.

injunction   Court order requiring that certain action not be taken.

keelboat   Boat without a sail used in shallow waterways such as rivers, propelled by oars. Generally used for carrying cargo, not people.

militia   Group of citizens trained as an army but not part of any official military force, usually used in emergencies.

Moravian   Protestant Christian denomination begun in the fifteenth century in Moravia, a part of Austria.

oblivion   State of being completely forgotten or nonexistent.

surveyor   Person who maps and marks land, roads, mines, and other physical geographic features.

syllabary   System of writing a language in which each character represents the sound of a syllable.

unilateral   Done by only one party.

wigwam   Rounded or cone-shaped Indian home or lodge made of poles covered with bark or animal hides.

FOR MORE INFORMATION

Cherokee Cultural Society
4407 Rose Street
Houston, TX 77007
Web site: http://www.powersource.com/cherokee/default.html

Cherokee National Historical Society
Cherokee Heritage Center and National Museum
P.O. Box 515
Tahlequah, OK 74465-0515
(918) 456-6007
Web site: http://www.powersource.com/heritage

National Trail of Tears Association
1100 North University Avenue, Suite 143
Little Rock, AR 72207-6344
(800) 441-4513
(501) 666-9032
Web site: http://rosecity.net/tears/trail/association

Web Sites

Due to the changing nature of Internet links, the Rosen Publishing Group, Inc., has developed an online list of Web sites related to the subject of this book. This site is updated regularly. Please use this link to access the list:

http://www.rosenlinks.com/psah/trte

# FOR FURTHER READING

Bealer, Alex W. *Only the Names Remain: The Cherokees and the Trail of Tears*. New York: Little Brown and Co., 1996.

Bruchac, Joseph. *The Journal of Jesse Smoke: A Cherokee Boy, Trail of Tears, 1838*. New York: Scholastic, 2001.

Cornelissen, Cornelia. *Soft Rain: A Story of the Cherokee Trail of Tears*. New York: Laureleaf, 1999.

Fremon, David K. *Trail of Tears*. Needham Heights, MA: Silver Burdett, 1994.

Glancy, Diane. *Pushing the Bear: A Novel of the Trail of Tears*. New York: Harvest Books, 1998.

Green, Michael D., ed. *The Cherokee Removal: A Brief History with Documents*. New York: Bedford/St. Martin's, 1995.

Hoig, Stanley. *Night of the Cruel Moon: Cherokee Removal and the Trail of Tears*. New York: Checkmark Books, 1996.

Kallen, Stuart A., and Cathryn J. Long. *The Cherokee*. Farmington Hills, MI: Gale Group, 2000.

Sanders, Evelin. *Cherokee Windsong*. New York: Royal Fireworks, 1996.

Stein, R. Conrad. *The Trail of Tears*. Chicago: Children's Press, 1995.

Underwood, Thomas, adapter. *Cherokee Legends and the Trail of Tears*. Cherokee, NC: Cherokee Publications, 1997.

Underwood, Thomas B., and Jacob Anchutin. *The Story of the Cherokee People*. Cherokee, NC: Cherokee Publications, 1996.

BIBLIOGRAPHY

"A Brief History of the Trail of Tears." The Cherokee Nation. 1998–2002. Retrieved October 2002 (http://www.cherokee.org/Culture/HistoryPage.asp?ID=2).

"Cherokee Removal Forts." About North Georgia. 1997. Retrieved October 2002 (http://ngeorgia.com/history/cherokeeforts.html).

Ehle, John. *Trail of Tears: The Rise and Fall of the Cherokee Nation.* New York: Anchor, 1989.

Golden, Randy. "The Trail of Tears." Our Georgia History. 2001–2002. Retrieved October 2002 (http://ourgeorgiahistory.com/indians/cherokee/trail_of_tears.html).

"Indian Removal." PBS Online. 1998. Retrieved October 2002 (http://www.pbs.org/wgbh/aia/part4/4p2959.html).

Jahoda, Gloria. *The Trail of Tears.* San Antonio: Wings Press, 1995.

Kappler, Charles J. *Indian Affairs: Laws and Treaties.* New York: AMS Press, Inc., 1996.

Mails, Thomas E. *The Cherokee People: A Story of the Cherokee from Earliest Origins to Contemporary Times.* New York: Marlowe and Company, 1996.

Moulton, Gary E., ed. *The Papers of Chief John Ross.* 2 vols. Norman, OK: University of Oklahoma Press, 1985.

"Records of the United States Senate (Record Group 46), 1789–1990." National Archives Research Room. 2003. Retrieved March 2003 (http://www.archives.gov/research_room/federal/_records_guide/us_senate_rg046.html).

Remini, Robert B. *Andrew Jackson and His Indian Wars.* New York: Viking, 2001.

"Scott's Address to the Cherokees," *Niles' National Register*, June 2, 1838, p. 210.

"The Trail of Tears." About North Georgia. 1997. Retrieved October 2002 (http://ngeorgia.com/history/nghisttt.html).

PRIMARY SOURCE IMAGE LIST

Page 9: A 1747 map by Emanuel Bowen entitled "A New & Accurate Map of the Provinces of North & South Carolina Georgia &c." Housed in the Hargrett Rare Book and Manuscript Library of the University of Georgia.

Page 11: A lithograph chart showing the Cherokee Syllabary invented by Sequoyah, c. 1835. Courtesy of Corbis.

Page 11 (inset): A c. 1836 hand-colored lithograph entitled *Se-Quo-Yah* published in Philadelphia by F. W. Greenough. Courtesy of the Prints and Photographs Division of the Library of Congress.

Page 14: A letter from President George Washington to the U.S. Senate concerning the Cherokee, dated August 11, 1790. Housed in the Library of Congress.

Page 14 (inset): A 1796 oil portrait of President George Washington by Gilbert Stuart. Courtesy of Francis G. Mayer/Corbis.

Page 17 (left): President Thomas Jefferson's confidential message to Congress concerning relations with the Indians, dated January 18, 1803. Housed in the National Archives.

Page 17 (right): An early-nineteenth-century portrait of Thomas Jefferson by Gilbert Stuart. Courtesy of the New York Historical Society.

Page 20: A c. 1830-1837 lithograph entitled *Andrew Jackson [with Indians]*. Housed in the William L. Clements Library, the University of Michigan.

Page 22: The Treaty with the Cherokee—1816, also known as the Turkey Town Treaty, signed on September 14, 1816. Courtesy of the Library of Congress.

Page 27: An illustrated paper wrapper for a book entitled *Narrative of the Capture and Providential Escape of Misses Frances and Almira Hall*, published in New York in 1835. Housed in the Rare Book and Special Collections Division of the Library of Congress.

Page 28: A lithograph by McKenney & Hall of John Ross, principal chief of the Cherokee, c. 1843. Published in Philadelphia by Daniel Rice & James G. Clark. Housed in the Prints and Photographs Division of the Library of Congress.

Page 29: A publication authored by John Ross entitled *Letter from John Ross, Principal Chief of the Cherokee Nation of Indians, in Answer to Inquiries from a Friend Regarding the Cherokee Affairs with the United States, Followed by a Copy of the Protest of the Cherokee Delegation.* The text of the protest was presented to Congress on June 21, 1836. Housed in the Hargrett Rare Book and Manuscript Library of the University of Georgia.

Page 31 (bottom): An 1832 Georgia lottery record for the home and property of John Ridge, drawn by Griffin Mathis. Courtesy of the Georgia Department of Archives and History.

Page 33: A portrait of Chief Justice John Marshall by John B. Martin. Courtesy of the Supreme Court of the United States, Office of the Curator.

Page 35 (top left): President Andrew Jackson's message to Congress "On Indian Removal," dated December 6, 1830. Courtesy of the National Archives.

Page 35 (bottom right): An 1884 map by C. C. Royce entitled "Map Showing the Territory Originally Assigned to the Cherokee 'Nation' of Indians." Housed in the Geography and Map Division of the Library of Congress.

Page 39: The Treaty of New Echota, signed on December 29, 1835, by General William Carroll and John F. Schermerhorn, commissioners on the part of the United States, and the "Chiefs Head Men and People of the Cherokee tribe of Indians." Courtesy of the National Archives.

Page 42: An 1847 lithograph of Winfield Scott by Currier & Ives. Courtesy of the Prints and Photographs Division of the Library of Congress.

Page 49: A photograph of General Stand Watie, c. 1860-1865. Housed in the National Archives. Courtesy of CORBIS.

Page 51: An 1875 photograph. On its back are written the words "Graduating class 1875, Cherokee Young Ladies Seminary, Park Hill, Indian Territory. Cost $45,000, built by the tribe without U.S. Government aid, fruits of Christian civilization." From the Collection of the Denver Public Library. Courtesy of the Library of Congress.

INDEX

About the Author

Ann Byers is a teacher, youth worker, thesis editor, and writer who lives in Fresno, California. Her husband and four grown children enjoy reading her books.

Photo Credits

Front cover, back cover (bottom left), Woolaroc Museum, Bartlesville, Oklahoma; back cover (top left and bottom right), pp. 1, 11 (bottom), 28, 42 Library of Congress, Prints and Photographs Division; back cover (top right) National Park Service, artist, Keith Rocco; back cover (middle right) Louisiana State Museum, gift of Dr. and Mrs. E. Ralph Lupin; pp. 9, 29 The Hargrett Rare Book and Manuscript Library, University of Georgia Libraries; p. 10 courtesy Chief Vann House Historic Site; p. 11 (top) © Corbis; p. 14 Library of Congress, Manuscript Division; p. 14 (inset) © Francis G. Mayer/Corbis; pp. 17 (left), 22, 39 National Archives and Records Administration; p. 17 (right) collection of the New-York Historical Society; p. 20 Clements Library, University of Michigan; p. 27 Library of Congress, Rare Book and Special Collections Division; p. 31 (top) courtesy of Chieftains Museum, Rome, Georgia; p. 31 (bottom) courtesy of Georgia Archives; p. 33 Vic Boswell/Collection of the Supreme Court of the United States; p. 35 (top) Records of the United States Senate, National Archives and Records Administration; p. 35 (bottom) Library of Congress, Geography and Map Division; p. 37 Marian Bailey Presswood/Polk County Historical & Genealogical Society; p. 45 Western National Parks Association; p. 49 Mathew Brady Studio/National Archives and Records Administration; p. 51 Denver Public Library, Western History Collection #X-32644; p. 52 courtesy of Cherokee Heritage Center, Tahlequah, Oklahoma.

Designer: Nelson Sá; Photo Researcher: Amy Feinberg